Healthy Eating

LEVEL 10

Teaching Tips

White Level 10

This book focuses on developing reading independence, fluency, and comprehension.

Before Reading

- Ask readers what they think the book will be about based on the title. Have them support their answer.

Read the Book

- Encourage readers to read silently on their own.
- As readers encounter unfamiliar words, ask them to look for context clues to see if they can figure out what the words mean. Encourage them to locate boldfaced words in the glossary and ask questions to clarify the meaning of new vocabulary.
- Allow readers time to absorb the text and think about each chapter.
- Ask readers to write down any questions they have about the book's content.

After Reading

- Ask readers to summarize the book.
- Encourage them to point out anything they did not understand and ask questions.
- Ask readers to review the questions on page 23. Have them go back through the book to find answers. Have them write their answers on a separate sheet of paper.

© 2024 Booklife Publishing
This edition is published by arrangement with Booklife Publishing.

North American adaptations © 2024 Jump!
5357 Penn Avenue South
Minneapolis, MN 55419
www.jumplibrary.com

Decodables by Jump! are published by Jump! Library.

Library of Congress Cataloging-in-Publication Data is available at www.loc.gov or upon request from the publisher.

ISBN: 979-8-88524-808-2 (hardcover)
ISBN: 979-8-88524-809-9 (paperback)
ISBN: 979-8-88524-810-5 (ebook)

Photo Credits

Images are courtesy of Shutterstock.com. With thanks to Getty Images, Thinkstock Photo and iStockphoto. Cover – karelnoppe. p4–5 –fizkes, Monkey Business Images. p6–7 -ifong, Hurst Photo. p8–9 – tinokoloski, Oleksandra Naumenko. p10–11 –Syda Productions, Antonina Vlasova. p12–13 – Prostock-studio. p14–15 –marilyn barbone, Antonina Vlasova. p16–17 - AnnGaysorn, Sudarshan negi. p18–19 - Yuliasis, Dmytro Zinkevych. p20–21 - Zaitsava Olga, LightField Studios.

Table of Contents

Page 4   Healthy Eating

Page 6   What Is Healthy Eating?

Page 8   Fruits and Vegetables

Page 9   Carbohydrates

Page 10   Sugars

Page 11   Fats

Page 12   Protein

Page 14   Minerals

Page 15   Vitamins

Page 16   Water

Page 18   A Balanced Diet

Page 20   Believe It or Not!

Page 21   Activity

Page 22   Index

Page 23   Questions

Page 24   Glossary

Healthy Eating

Our bodies are amazing machines. They help us work, rest, and play. Any machine needs fuel to work. You put gas in a car and batteries in toys. Your body needs fuel too.

Our bodies are all different and are all good at different things. What is your body good at?

Food doesn't just give us **energy**, though. Food helps our bodies heal if we are hurt. While we are still children, our bodies are also growing and changing all the time. The right foods have all the things you need to help your body do this.

What Is Healthy Eating?

Eating lots of different foods helps us get all the **nutrients** we need. Foods with similar nutrients are arranged in groups, and we call these the food groups.

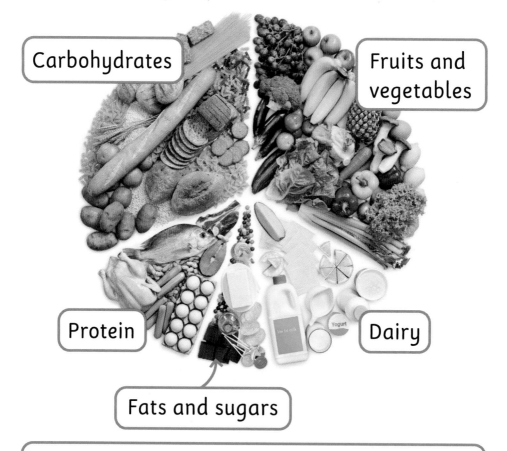

Carbohydrates

Fruits and vegetables

Protein

Dairy

Fats and sugars

Some people don't eat food that comes from animals. They might eat plant-based foods instead, such as tofu.

Having a balanced diet is important for staying healthy. A balanced diet includes food from all the different groups.

You should try and eat at least five portions of fruits and vegetables each day. Some people aim for as many as ten!

Fruits and Vegetables

Fruits and vegetables grow from plants and give us lots of **vitamins**, **minerals**, and **fiber**. For every meal, you should try to fill half of your plate with fruits and vegetables of different colors.

Fruits and vegetables are usually full of fiber.

Carbohydrates

Carbohydrates, often called carbs, give us energy. Simple carbs can be found in fruit, milk, and sweet foods. They are broken down quickly by the body and used for a quick energy boost. Complex carbs take longer to break down. They give us a slower boost of energy, but it lasts longer.

Sugars

Sugars are simple carbs and taste sweet. They can be found naturally in milk, fruits, and vegetables or can be added to foods to make them taste sweeter. A little bit of sugar, especially the kind found in fruit and milk, is OK in your diet. However, too much sugar can be unhealthy.

Fats

Fats help our bodies store energy for when we might need it later. A little fat in our diets is important. However, saturated fats are not good for our hearts and can be found in lots of different foods.

Protein

Protein is needed for the body to be able to repair itself and grow. Our bodies use protein to repair **muscles** after exercise. People who exercise often need to eat more protein to help their muscles recover.

You should try to eat two portions of fish each week.

Some people choose not to eat meat. These people are called vegetarians. Others choose not to use any animal products at all. These people are called vegans. People might choose this for health or for religious or ethical reasons. Vegetarians and vegans get their protein from healthy plant-based foods instead.

Minerals

Minerals help our bodies grow and heal. They are often found in the ground, and small amounts of them end up in foods. The body needs the right amount to be able to use other nutrients properly. If you don't eat enough minerals, your body can become weak and tired.

Vitamins

Vitamins are nutrients found in the foods we eat. Our bodies need vitamins to work properly. Each type of food contains different types of vitamins. Some foods contain one type, while other foods contain many types. This is why it is important to eat a varied diet. The more types of food you eat, the more vitamins you get.

Water

Humans, like all living things, need water to live. Our bodies are over 60 percent water, but we lose water when we breathe, sweat, or go to the bathroom. We can replace this missing water by drinking and eating. Water is the healthiest way to do this.

If we do not drink enough water, we become **dehydrated**. This can make us feel very ill very quickly. You can tell if you are drinking enough. How? You will not feel thirsty, and your urine will be a very pale yellow color.

A Balanced Diet

It is important to know that there are no "good" or "bad" foods—just foods we should enjoy lots of and foods we only need a little of. Making sure we get all our carbs, protein, fats, vitamins, and minerals in the right amounts will give our bodies what they need to work.

While you are still growing, it is important to give your body what it needs. Growing up is a lot of work!

Remember to try to eat five portions of different fruits and vegetables each day.

A portion is usually what fits in the palm of your hand.

Believe It or Not!

Is a tomato a fruit or a vegetable? Many people would say it is a vegetable. They certainly wouldn't put tomatoes in a fruit salad. Scientists say that a fruit is the part of the plant that has the seeds inside. A tomato has seeds, so it is a fruit.

Activity

Can you plan a balanced meal for you and everyone at home? Think about your favorite meals. Then try to make sure they are balanced. Do you have some protein, some carbs, some fruits, and vegetables?

Index

balanced diets 7, 21

fats 6, 11, 18

fruit 7–10, 19–21

minerals 8, 14, 18

proteins 6, 12–13, 18, 21

sugars 6, 10

vegetables 7–8, 10, 13, 19–21

vitamins 8, 15, 18

How to Use an Index

An index helps us find information in a book. Each word has a set of page numbers. These page numbers are where you can find information about that word.

Page numbers

Example: balloons 5, 8–10, 19

Important word

This means page 8, page 10, and all the pages in between. Here, it means pages 8, 9, and 10.

Questions

1. What is an example of a protein food?

2. How many portions of fruits and vegetables should you eat each day?

3. What percentage of our bodies is water?

4. Can you use the Table of Contents to find out what carbohydrates are also called?

5. Can you use the Index to find information about minerals in the book?

6. Using the Glossary, can you define what energy is?

Glossary

dehydrated:
Lacking enough water in the body for normal function.

energy:
The ability or strength to do things without getting tired.

fiber:
A part of fruits, vegetables, and grains that passes through the body and helps move food through the intestines.

minerals:
Solid substances that are found in Earth that our bodies need to stay healthy.

muscles:
Tissues in the body that connect to bones to make them move.

nutrients:
Substances our bodies need to stay strong and healthy.

vitamins:
Substances in food that our bodies need for good health and nutrition.